This book belongs to:

....

First published in 2015 by Alison Green Books
An imprint of Scholastic Children's Books
Euston House, 24 Eversholt Street
London NW1 1DB
A division of Scholastic Ltd
www.scholastic.co.uk
London – New York – Toronto – Sydney – Auckland
Mexico City – New Delhi – Hong Kong

Based on *The Highway Rat*, the original picture book
by Julia Donaldson and Axel Scheffler

Text copyright © 2011 Julia Donaldson
Illustrations copyright © 2011 and 2015 Axel Scheffler

ISBN: 978 1 407155 74 6

1 3 5 7 9 8 6 4 2

Papers used by Scholastic Children's Books are made from
wood grown in sustainable forests.

The Highway Rat
Activity Book

By Julia Donaldson

Illustrated by Axel Scheffler

ALISON GREEN BOOKS

Stand and Deliver!

Can you colour in this picture of
the Highway Rat and his horse?

The Highway Rat is Lost!

Which path will lead the Highway Rat out of the cave?

Yum, Yum!

Who's eating all the buns and biscuits?
Join the dots to find out.

Galloping down the road

There are four pieces missing from this jigsaw. They're all in the sticker section at the back of the book. Find them and complete the jigsaw.

Crunchy Slaw

The Highway Rat loves vegetables.

Why don't you make this recipe to share?

It's perfect for a picnic!

---

1. Wash and peel all of the fruit and vegetables
2. Grate them all into a large bowl. If you have one, you can use the grater attachment on a food processor.
3. Mix in the oil and lemon juice and stir well.
4. Add the yogurt a spoonful at a time, tasting until you have a flavour that you like.

You will need:

3 carrots

2 raw beetroots

2 apples

½ a white cabbage

1 tbsp olive oil

Juice of ½ a lemon

1-3 tbsp Greek yogurt

Grater

Large bowl

Vegetable peeler

Always ask a grown-up for help when you're using kitchen utensils.

Match the Shadow

Can you match the shadows to the right pictures?

You will need:

Coloured tissue paper
(about 2 large sheets)
Small plastic pot with lid
(a hummus/yogurt pot or similar)
PVA glue
Double-sided tape
Sticky tape
Cardboard or stiff card
Coloured paper/wrapping paper
Paint
Paintbrush
Glitter
Beads

Trick or Treat!

Fool the Highway Rat by hiding all your treats in this colourful cake box.

1. Draw around the lid of your plastic pot on to the cardboard or stiff card and cut out the outlined circle.

2. Scrunch together half of a sheet of tissue paper into a ball and tape to the card circle.

3. Now cut the remaining tissue paper into long strips, roughly 3cm wide.

4. Twist the strips of tissue as seen below.

Always ask a grown-up to help when you're using scissors

5. Secure one end of a twisted strip under the cardboard disc with sticky tape.

6. Cover the ball of tissue with PVA glue and begin to wind the twist of tissue around it.

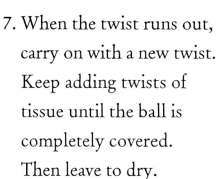

7. When the twist runs out, carry on with a new twist. Keep adding twists of tissue until the ball is completely covered. Then leave to dry.

8. Whilst your tissue is drying, cover the plastic pot with coloured paper or wrapping paper using sticky tape. Alternatively, you can use plain paper and paint it whatever colour you like.

9. Once the tissue is dry, paint the top whatever colour you would like your cake to be. Add glitter or other decorations by sprinkling them on to the wet paint.

10. When the paint has dried, attach the tissue cake top to the lid of the decorated pot with double-sided tape.

11. If you like, you can make a cherry to go on top by scrunching a small ball of tissue and covering it with some smooth tissue as shown in the pictures below. Then glue it to the top of your cake with PVA glue.

Picnic Time!

Can you colour in this picture?

Highway Rat Bunting

You will need: scissors, glue,
1.5m string, ribbon or cotton

1. Cut around all the coloured triangles.
2. Fold along all the dotted lines.
3. Take one triangle. Carefully glue along the tab at the top, then fold it over the string or ribbon, starting 15cm from the end.
4. Repeat with all the triangles until you have a lovely string of bunting to hang in your room!
   (See picture overleaf.)

Always ask a grown-up to help when you're using scissors

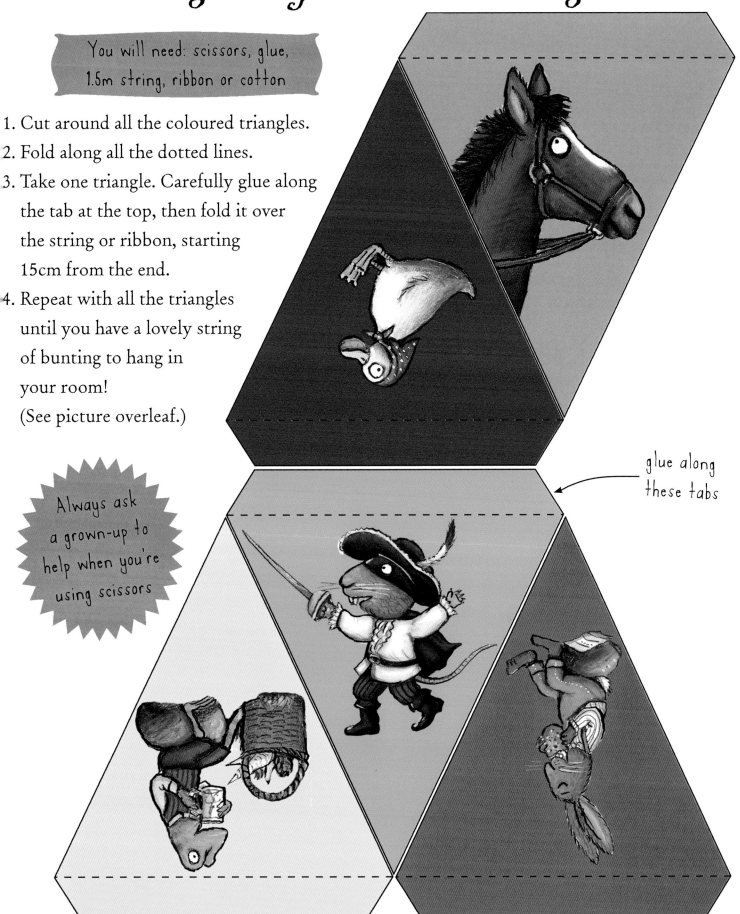

glue along these tabs

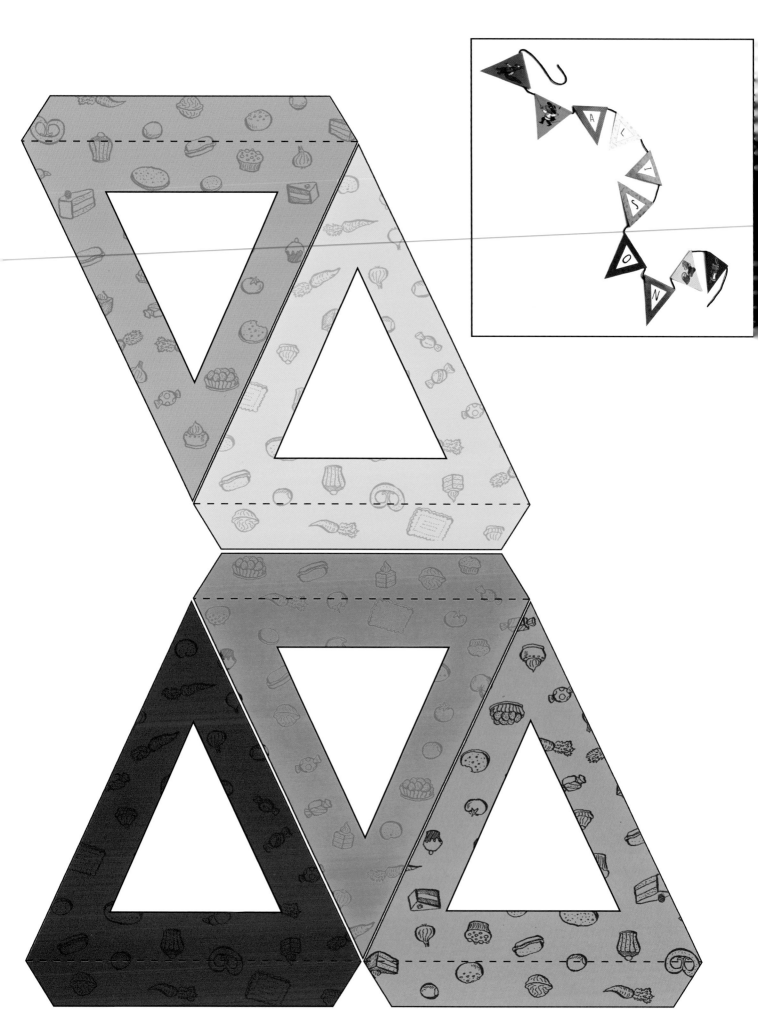

Draw a picture in the white spaces, or write your name, putting one letter in each triangle.

Who goes there?

Who's this hopping along the road?
Join the dots to solve the mystery.

Tasty Treat wordsearch

There are five foods hidden in this wordsearch. One of them has been circled for you – can you find the other four?

C	L	O	V	E	R
A	N	P	I	L	O
R	U	C	A	K	E
R	T	P	R	V	A
O	S	A	J	T	K
T	O	M	A	T	O

CAKE

NUTS

CARROT

TOMATO

CLOVER
(already circled)

Halt!

Can you colour in this picture of the Highway Rat
stealing the rabbit's clover?

School

Can you help the Highway Rat with his lessons?

Can you do the sums?

$1 + 3 =$

$4 - 1 =$

Can you count how many cakes the Highway Rat has stolen?

Answer:

Orange

Red

Pink

Green

Brown

Can you match the colours to the food?

Can you match the pairs?

Which one is the odd one out?

A. B. C. D.

Answer: D is the odd one out

Can you trace the names of the animals?

frog rat

duck

You will need:

For the cakes:
110g softened butter
110g caster sugar
2 eggs
1 tsp vanilla extract
110g/4oz self-raising flour
1-2 tbsp milk

For the icing:
140g softened butter
280g icing sugar
1-2 tbsp milk
Green food colouring

For decorating:
Desiccated coconut mixed with
    green food colouring
Packet of chocolate discs with
    hard chocolate shells
Small tube of chocolate icing
12 mint leaves (optional)

Mixing bowl
Whisk (hand or electric)
Cupcake cases
Muffin tin
Wire rack
Sieve

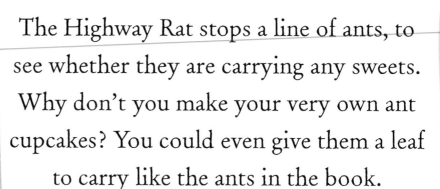

Ant Cupcakes

The Highway Rat stops a line of ants, to see whether they are carrying any sweets. Why don't you make your very own ant cupcakes? You could even give them a leaf to carry like the ants in the book.

To make your cakes:

Preheat the oven to 180°C/380°F/Gas 4.

1. In a large bowl, whisk the sugar and butter together till they are light and fluffy.
2. Break the eggs into the bowl and add the vanilla extract.
3. Sift in the flour, and mix together.
4. Stir in the milk.
5. Place the cupcake cases in a muffin tin and fill each one about two-thirds full.
6. Cook for 10-15 minutes. The cakes will turn golden-brown when ready.
7. Place the cupcakes on a wire rack and leave to cool.

Makes about
12 cakes

To make the icing:

1. In a bowl, add the milk to the softened butter.
2. Gradually sift in the icing sugar and beat it all together until the mixture is light and fluffy.
3. Pour a few drops of green food colouring into the mixture, and stir together.

To decorate your cakes:

1. Smooth the icing on to each cupcake using a spoon.
2. Roll the edges of the cupcakes in the desiccated coconut.
3. Line up three chocolate discs on the top of each cake.
4. Now, using the tube of chocolate icing, pipe three legs coming out of the central disc.
5. Add two blobs of icing on the head of your ant for antennae.
6. Finally, stick a mint leaf on to the ant with a dab of icing.

Always ask a grown-up to help you when you're cooking

What's Next?

Can you circle what comes next in each of the patterns below?

Neigh!

Who carries the Highway Rat as he steals everyone's food?
Join the dots to find out.

Spot the Difference

There are five differences between these two pictures.

Can you spot them all?

Answers: The horse's saddle has vanished, as has the moon from the sky. The duck has appeared and is eating by the fireside. The owl perching on the branch has changed to a crow, and the dancing squirrel's waistcoat has changed from blue to pink.

Finding his way

Can you colour in this picture of the Highway Rat exploring the echoey cave?

You will need:

- 1 pair of large socks
- 1 wrapping paper tube
- 1 rectangular piece of felt
- 1 pipecleaner
- 1 elastic band
- Bubble wrap
- White paint
- Black paint
- Paintbrush
- PVA glue
- Ribbon
- Coloured tissue paper
- Scissors

Clip Clop!

Make your very own hobby horse!

Always ask a grown-up to help when you're using scissors

1. Paint the cardboard tube with a layer of PVA glue and cover with the coloured tissue paper and leave to dry. You can alternate colours to make stripes.

2. While the tube is drying, stuff one sock with bubble wrap until it is rigid. This will be your horse's head.

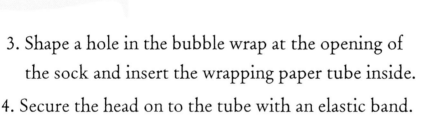

3. Shape a hole in the bubble wrap at the opening of the sock and insert the wrapping paper tube inside.

4. Secure the head on to the tube with an elastic band.

5. Cut two diamond shapes from the other sock. These will become your horse's ears. To shape them, pinch one end and glue it together as seen in the picture below.

6. Allow to dry, then glue to either side of the head.

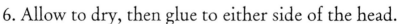

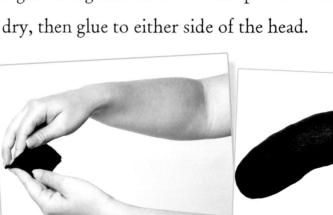

6. To make the mane, fold the felt rectangle in half. Use scissors to cut three-quarters of the way in, leaving 2 cm on each side of the fold. Continue this all the way down the rectangle at 3 cm intervals.

7. Glue the mane along the neck of the horse, as seen in the picture on the right.

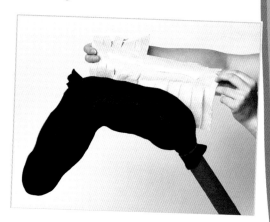

8. Use the paint to give your horse eyes, nostrils and a smile.

9. Now, use the pipe cleaner as a harness, by wrapping it around the horse's nose.

10. Finally, thread a ribbon through the pipe cleaner and tie the ends. These are your horse's reins.

You can use extra bits of felt to add a forelock or a blaze to your horse - just cut them out and glue them on!

The Highway Rat

There are four pieces missing from this jigsaw.
They're all in the sticker section at the back of the book.
Can you find them and complete the scene?

Animal wordsearch

There are five animals hidden in this wordsearch. One has already been circled for you – can you find the other four?

DUCK
(already circled)

RAT

S	P	I	D	E	R
F	D	I	R	L	A
R	D	U	C	K	B
O	F	K	E	R	B
G	R	O	N	G	I
W	T	S	R	A	T

RABBIT

SPIDER

FROG

Spot the Difference

There are five differences between these two scenes.

Can you spot them all?

Feasting all night long

Can you colour in this picture of the animals celebrating?

Quack! Quack!

Who waddles down the road and outwits the Highway Rat?
Find out by joining the dots!

Honey and Apple Juice

You will need:

2-3 tbsps of
    boiling water

5cm cinnamon stick

1/4 tsp cinnamon powder

3 heaped tsps of honey

250ml of fresh apple juice

10 ice cubes

Heatproof container

Blender (optional)

Sieve

The Highway Rat steals some clover from a rabbit. Did you know that bees can make honey from clover? Why don't you make this delicious honey and apple juice drink to share?

1. Ask an adult to pour the hot water into a heatproof bowl and add the cinnamon stick. Infuse together for about 5 minutes.

2. Whilst the water is still hot, stir in the cinnamon powder and honey.

3. Put some ice cubes into a blender along with the apple juice and cinnamon mixture and blend together until smooth. If you don't have a blender, just put the ice into a glass and follow on to the next step.

4. Pour the liquid into a serving glass through a sieve and decorate with a slice of fruit.

Always ask a grown-up for help when you're using kitchen utensils.

A cake shop!

Can you colour in this picture of the cake shop?

Finger Puppets

Act out your own Highway Rat stories with these finger puppets.

Always ask a grown-up to help when you're using scissors

cut along the dotted lines

Wrap these tabs around your finger and fasten with sticky tape.

A new job!

Join the dots to find out who's sweeping the cake shop's floor.

Hay-Bale Treats

The Highway Rat steals his own horse's hay. Can you make some hay-bale treats to replace the ones the Highway Rat has stolen?

You will need:

For the treats:

3 tbsps butter

180g Marshmallows (large or small)

6 cups puffed rice cereal

For the icing and decorating:

70g softened butter

140g icing sugar

1 tbsp milk

Yellow food colouring

200g Desiccated coconut

A shallow pan, approx. 30 x 20 x 5cm

Saucepan

Mixing Bowl

Whisk (hand or electric)

Wooden Spoon

Frying pan

Sieve

To make your treats:

1. Melt the butter in a large saucepan over a low heat.
2. Add the marshmallows and stir until they are completely melted. Take the saucepan off the heat.
3. Stir in the puffed rice until it is completely coated in the marshmallow mixture.
4. Using a wooden spoon, press the mixture into a greased pan.
5. Cool in the fridge for at least two hours.

Always ask a grown-up to help you when you're cooking

To make the icing:

1. In a bowl, add the milk to the softened butter.

2. Sift in the icing sugar and beat it all together until the mixture is light and fluffy.

3. Pour a few drops of yellow food colouring into the mixture, and stir together.

To decorate:

1. Toast the desiccated coconut in a frying pan over a medium heat. It will turn a golden colour when ready.

2. Transfer the coconut to a plate and allow to cool.

3. Once cool, mix in a few drops of yellow food colouring until you have a hay-like colour.

4. Now, spread the icing over the rice treats and roll them in the coconut until they are completely covered.

5. Stack your hay-bale treats in a tower – they're ready to eat!

Makes eight to ten treats

Lost Duck!

Can you help the duck avoid the Highway Rat and find her way back to her feasting friends?

F.
E.
D.
C.
B.
A.

Nibble! Nibble!

Who's this holding a sack of nuts? Join the dots to solve the mystery.

Who's Who?

Can you work out who is who by matching
the whole picture to their fragment?

Drawing Fun!

Draw the characters by copying each square of the left-hand grid into the blank grid on the right.

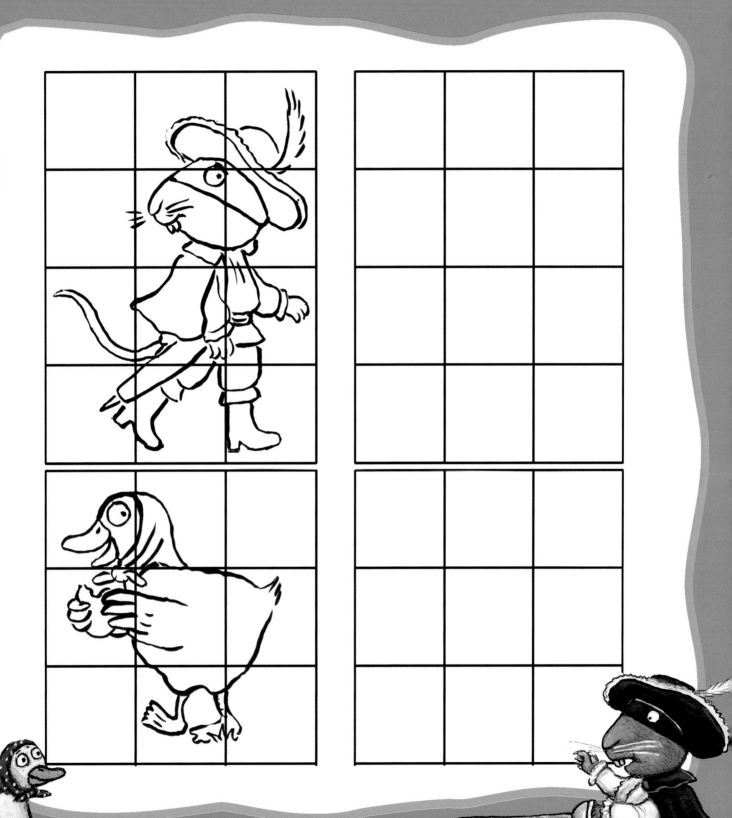

You will need:

A cup of rice
A sturdy cardboard tube
A sheet of card the same width as the cardboard tube
Cardboard
Sticky tape
Double-sided tape
Jug/funnel
Pen
Scissors
Paint
Paintbrushes

Make some noise!

When all the animals are having fun round the campfire they like to play their musical instruments. Why don't you make a colourful shaker so you can join in, too?

1. Place the tube on the cardboard and draw around the end twice, making two circles.
2. Cut out the two cardboard circles.
3. Secure one of the circles over one end of the tube with sticky tape.
4. Turn the tube upside down so the uncovered end is pointing upwards and pour in the rice using a jug or funnel.
5. Now secure the other cardboard circle over the uncovered end with sticky tape so that no rice can escape.

6. Stick a strip of double-sided tape to the cardboard tube and attach the edge of the sheet of card to it.

7. Roll the card around the tube partway before adding another strip of double-sided tape.

8. Keep turning the tube and adding more strips of double-sided tape until the tube is wrapped in card approximately 3 times.

9. When completely covered, decorate your shaker by painting it as you like.

10. Once dry, your shaker is ready to use!

Top Tip:
You could use the stickers at the back of this book to decorate your shaker!

How many...

... animals have their eyes closed?

... musical instruments can you see?

... rabbits are at the feast?

... ants can you count?

These are the stickers for the "Galloping Down the Road" Jigsaw.

These are the stickers to decorate your cake with.

These are the stickers for the "The Highway Rat" Jigsaw.